The Majesty of
ST. AUGUSTINE

By
Steven Brooke

PELICAN PUBLISHING COMPANY
Gretna 2005

for Suzanne and Miles
Annie, Merlin, Max, and Clifford

The word "Pelican" and the depiction of a pelican are trademarks
of Pelican Publishing Company, Inc., and are registered in the
U.S. Patent and Trademark Office.

Library of Congress Cataloging-in-Publication Data

Brooke, Steven.
  The majesty of St. Augustine / by Steven Brooke.
      p. cm.
    ISBN 9781589802254 (hardcover : alk. paper)
  1. Historic buildings—Florida—Saint Augustine—Pictorial works. 2. Dwellings—
Florida—Saint Augustine—Pictorial works. 3. Historic sites—Florida—Saint
Augustine—Pictorial works. 4. Saint Augustine (Fla.)—Buildings, structures, etc.—
Pictorial works. 5. Architecture—Florida—Saint Augustine—Pictorial works. I. Title.

  F319.S2B76 2005
  975.9'18—dc22

                                                        2004017083

Printed in Korea
Published by Pelican Publishing Company, Inc.
1000 Burmaster Street, Gretna, Louisiana 70053

Contents

The Bridge of Lions with a view to Anastasia Island.

Acknowledgments

I am grateful to Leslie Keyes, Sally Ann Freeman, Brian Thompson, Andrew Lekos, Annamarie Smith, Michele Blevins, Jay Humphries, and Judy Allen for their invaluable assistance with the photography. I extend my thanks to Dr. William Adams for his suggestions and assistance with the research. My sincere thanks go to Karen Keep for my stay at the Panther Lodge on Anastasia Island. As always, I extend my gratitude to Dr. Milburn Calhoun, president of Pelican Publishing Company, for his continued support of my work.

History of St. Augustine

St. Augustine, Florida, the oldest European settlement in the United States, is situated on the Atlantic coast in a narrow peninsula formed by the Sebastian and Matanzas Rivers, on the west side of a harbor which is separated from the ocean by the low and narrow island of Anastasia. It lies about forty miles south of the mouth of the St. John's River, and about 160 miles south of Savannah, Georgia.

St. Augustine's turbulent and colorful history is generally divided into the following periods: *First Spanish Period*, 1556-1763; *British Decades*, 1763-1784; *Second Spanish Period*, 1784-1821; *Territorial Era*, 1821-1845; *Early Statehood*, 1845-1888; *Flagler's Golden Era*, 1888-1914; *Twentieth and Twenty-First Centuries*, 1914-present.

The Spaniards founded the city in 1565, more than half a century before the landing of the pilgrims at Plymouth. From its inception, St. Augustine was a nexus of geopolitical struggles.

Its founder, the eminent Spaniard Don Pedro Menéndez, was a commander during the reign of Philip II. Menéndez led an expedition to Florida consisting of thirty-four vessels and a crew of over two thousand. Their purpose was to colonize the region and suppress the Protestant French Huguenots who settled near the mouth of the St. John's in 1564. Menéndez landed at St. Augustine on August 28, 1565, and established his colony. He then marched to exterminate the Huguenots, putting to death all his prisoners, "not because they are Frenchmen, but because they are heretics and enemies of God."

Two years later, this massacre was avenged by a French adventurer, Dominique de Gourgues, who, with a small force of volunteers, attacked and captured the Spanish forts on the St. John's and hanged his prisoners, "not because they are Spanish, but because they are traitors, robbers, and murderers." de Gourgues made no attempt to retain his conquest; after extracting his retribution, he sailed back to France.

Menéndez was in Spain during this attack. His reputation earned him the rank of captain-general of the navy. His career in Florida, though stained with cruelty, was distinguished by energy and perseverance; and he is appropriately credited with establishing the first permanent settlement in the United States.

Menéndez's selection of St. Augustine as the site for his settlement showed good judgment. The harbor could accommodate supply vessels for the garrison, but was inaccessible to larger class ships, especially potential fleets of attack vessels. The estuaries and marshes on the landward side were a natural defense from Indian attack. More importantly, the region was surrounded by salt marshes. The prevailing sea breezes and salt air protected the colonists from diseases that proved fatal to the first settlers on the southern coasts of the United States.

In 1586, Sir Francis Drake, the legendary English navigator and privateer, returning from an expedition against the Spanish West Indies, appeared off the St. Augustine coast. He so terrified the Spaniards that they abandoned the fort and the town to him without resistance, fleeing to the shelter of the forts on the St. John's River. Drake took possession of the town, then pillaged and burned it, carrying away considerable treasure. The principal public buildings at that time were a courthouse, a church, and a monastery. After Drake's departure, the Spaniards returned and rebuilt the town. However, it grew so slowly that in 1647 there were within its walls only three hundred families, or fifteen hundred inhabitants, including fifty monks of the order of St. Francis.

In 1665, a party of English buccaneers, commanded by Capt. John Davis, launched an attack upon St. Augustine with seven small vessels. The two hundred man garrison was unable to resist the attack, which was probably initiated from the south by boats. To offset these attacks, the Spanish began construction of the Castillo de San Marcos. It was completed in the late 1600s, and none too soon as the British were poised to stage a major offensive.

In 1702, Spain and England were at war. An expedition against St. Augustine was organized by South Carolina's Governor Moore. It consisted of six hundred colonists, and as many Indian allies. The plan was to attack both by land and sea. The land force was commanded by Colonel Daniel, the naval force by Governor Moore. Daniel's forces reached St. Augustine before the naval expedition and easily captured the town. The governor, Don Joseph Cuniga, and the inhabitants took refuge in the castle, which was supplied with provisions and contained a considerable garrison. Governor Moore and the fleet arrived and attacked the fortification; but, without siege-guns of sufficient caliber, they made no impression on the coquina stone walls of the fort. Colonel Daniel was sent to Jamaica to procure heavier guns. In his absence, two Spanish vessels appeared off the harbor. Governor Moore feared that he was about to be attacked by a superior force. With his retreat cut off, he quickly raised the siege, destroyed whatever munitions he could not remove, and burned the town. He retreated by land, abandoning his vessels to the Spanish squadron whose appearance had alarmed him. Shortly afterward, Colonel Daniel

returned from Jamaica with mortars and heavy guns, but found Moore gone. Daniel, himself, was nearly captured. The expedition returned to Carolina in disgrace, but without the loss of a single man. It cost the colony of South Carolina six thousand pounds, and led to the issue of the first paper money ever circulated in America.

In 1727, Colonel Parker, an energetic officer, made a raid into Florida with about three hundred Carolina militia. He brought a wave of destruction to the gates of St. Augustine. Though he sacked a Yemassee village about a mile north of St. Augustine, he never attacked the city.

In 1740, Spain and England were again at war. An expedition against St. Augustine was organized by the famous Gen. James Oglethorpe, then governor of Georgia. He obtained assistance from South Carolina, and a naval force of six ships from England. On June 1, his forces reached St. Augustine, which was defended by a weakly manned garrison commanded

by Don Manuel de Monteano, the governor of Florida. After a siege of over six weeks, primarily by bombardment from Anastasia Island, Oglethorpe realized that he could not succeed. In anticipation of bad weather, he withdrew his fleet and sailed away on July 9.

Two years later, Governor Monteano, having received reinforcements from Cuba, sailed from St. Augustine with thirty-six vessels and three thousand men to attack the English settlements in Georgia. He met with some initial success, but was ultimately defeated by both Oglethorpe's forces and his military finesse. Monteano returned to Florida. In 1743, Oglethorpe made a raid into the Spanish dominions to the gates of St. Augustine. He advanced with such stealth that the Indians attached to his force captured and scalped forty Spanish troops under the walls of the Castillo de San Marcos.

The Treaty of Paris in 1763 established peace between Spain and England and ended the French and Indian War. Florida was ceded to the English in exchange for Havana, which had been taken by an English fleet during the war. This agreement was distasteful to the Floridians, and most went to Mexico and the West Indies. To offset this depopulation, the English promoted emigration to the newly acquired territory. An association was formed in London, headed by Scotsman Dr. Andrew Turnbull, who envisioned settling the large and valuable body of land lying near Mosquito Inlet. They proposed recruiting settlers from the south of Europe and the Mediterranean islands. The Minorcans, in particular, lived in a similar climate, and it was thought they would successfully relocate to the Florida shore. Accordingly, in 1767, fifteen hundred Greeks, Italians, and Minorcans emigrated to New Smyrna on the Mosquito Inlet ninety miles south of St. Augustine. They remained there until 1776 when disease reduced their numbers to about six hundred. Dissatisfied with their treatment by the proprietors of the colony, they abandoned New Smyrna and made their way to St. Augustine, where land was assigned to them in the northern part of the city.

The British kept possession of Florida until 1783 when the Second Treaty of Paris returned it to Spain in exchange for the Bahama Islands. At that time, St. Augustine had three thousand inhabitants. A few English families remained after the evacuation of the British as well as the entire settlement of Greeks and Minorcans, who had come up from Dr. Turnbull's colony on Mosquito Inlet. They were all Roman Catholics, accustomed to a language resembling Spanish, and not affected to any great degree by the change of rulers.

During the Second Spanish Period (1784-1821) Spain suffered the

Napoleonic invasions at home, and struggled to retain its New World colonies. Though Florida was no longer of prime importance to Spain, the expanding United States regarded the peninsula as vital to its interests.

In 1821, Florida passed from Spanish control to that of the United States. About three hundred buildings stood in the town. Florida remained a territory of the United States until 1845 when it was accepted into the union. The Territorial Period (1821-1845) was marked by an intense war with native Indians, the Second Seminole War. The United States Army took over the Castillo de San Marcos and renamed it Fort Marion.

When the Civil War broke out in 1861, Florida joined the Confederacy. Union troops occupied St. Augustine and held the city throughout the war.

By 1880, through the efforts of industrialist Henry Flagler, St. Augustine entered a period of great splendor. Flagler, a former partner of John D. Rockefeller in the Standard Oil Company, envisioned a retreat for the wealthy in St. Augustine. In 1886, his railroad company linked St. Augustine with the cities of the eastern seaboard. In 1887, he built two grand hotels and added a third the following year. The elaborate Mediterranean and Moorish Revival architecture of these buildings helped set the style for building throughout the state, especially in Palm Beach and Miami.

By the turn of the century, St. Augustine fell victim to the fickleness of the rich travelers and never achieved the status of other great resorts towns such as Newport, Rhode Island. St. Augustine did remain a tourist destination, particularly for the growing number of automobile travelers.

In 1965, St. Augustine celebrated its four hundredth anniversary. With this anniversary came a commitment from the state of Florida to restore the thirty-six surviving historic buildings. In 1997, St. Augustine assumed management and architectural control of the historic structures, thus ensuring that any architectural changes would respect the city's invaluable architectural heritage.

The Department of Heritage Tourism

The City of St. Augustine's Department of Heritage Tourism administers the city's seven-decade long program of preservation, restoration, and interpretation. The department's primary mission is the preservation of the historic resources entrusted to the City of St. Augustine by the State of Florida, the maintenance and expansion of the interpretation program centered on those resources, and continuation of efforts to restore a significant part of the colonial city. The department generates support from residents of the city and throughout the United States who value the city's historic resources and the contributions of Spain and Spanish-speaking people to the historical and cultural development of the United States.

The department manages the Colonial Spanish Quarter Museum, an interactive eighteenth-century living history museum that contains nine structures and is located in the heart of St. Augustine's Restoration Area. The department also manages library and archival holdings that contain maps, artwork, published volumes, photographs, archaeological research files, and site research on over twenty-five hundred buildings in the city.

MAP OF THE CITY

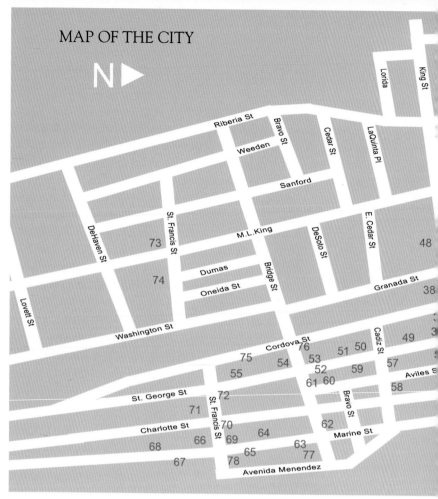

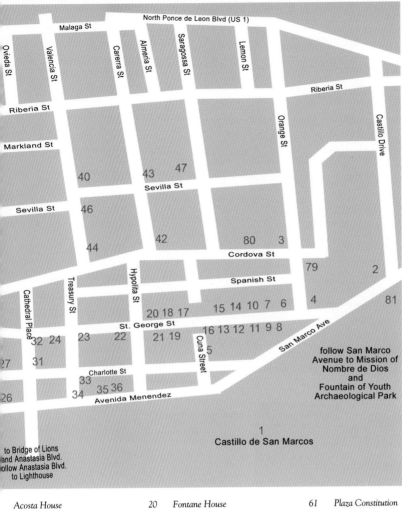

North Ponce de Leon Blvd (US 1)

Malaga St

Oviéda St
Valencia St
Carrera St
Almería St
Saragossa St
Lemon St

Riberia St

Riberia St

Orange St

Castillo Drive

Markland St

40   43   47

Sevilla St

Sevilla St   46

44   42   80   3

Cordova St

79   2

Hypolita St
Spanish St   81

Treasury St   20 18 17   15 14 10 7 6   4

Cathedral Place   St. George St

32 24   23   22   21 19   16 13 12 11 9 8

San Marco Ave

27   31

Cuna Street   5   follow San Marco
Avenue to Mission of
Nombre de Dios
and
Fountain of Youth
Archaeological Park

33
34   35 36

Charlotte St

26   Avenida Menendez

1
Castillo de San Marcos

to Bridge of Lions
and Anastasia Blvd.
follow Anastasia Blvd.
to Lighthouse

CASTILLO DE SAN MARCOS AND VICINITY

In 1672, Spain's Queen Regent Mariana ordered the construction of this stone fort to defend St. Augustine which was critical for the defense of the coast of Florida. Built of locally quarried coquina, a non-brittle soft shell, the walls were able to withstand cannon barrages. In 1702, British troops from South Carolina attacked the fort for fifty days. The siege failed and the British burned the town. The Spanish rebuilt the fort, reinforcing the northern side. In 1740, the British attacked again. After failing to breach the fort for twenty-seven days, they gave up.

Above: A view of the fort from the South. The watchtower overlooks the river. In 1842, the U. S. Army filled in the area behind the wall. Originally part of the moat, the water battery has cannon mounts which allow the cannon to fire over the wall.

Left: The City Wall was constructed of palm logs and earth. It ran from the Castillo westward to the San Sebastian River.

Center: The main entrance is accessible only with the draw bridge.

Right: To the right, the ravelin protects the drawbridge. The bastion is on the left.

St. Augustine Visitors Center: Architect Fred A. Hendricht (1879-1941) came to St. Augustine in 1905. A pioneer of the Mediterranean Revival style, he built hospitals, schools, and private residences. Located on San Marco Avenue, this structure was built in 1937 on the site of the old Hotel San Marco and features a stucco finish with coquina shells.

The Old Drug Store: Built in 1886, it was used by T. W. Speissegger and Sons until the 1960s. Located on the corner of Orange and Cordova Streets, it is now a museum.

The City Gates: The Spanish built the Cubo Defense Line in 1739. This gate was the only entry to the city from the north. In 1808, the walls were strengthened with stone and the coquina pillars were built.

Cuna Street: Cuna Street was laid out in the 1600s. It runs between Avenida Menéndez, near the Castillo de San Marcos, and Cordova Street. During the many periods of hostilities, pedestrians on Cuna Street walked within range of musket fire.

ST. GEORGE STREET

The City Gates, entrance to St. George Street: St. George Street is St. Augustine's main pedestrian thoroughfare. It was begun in 1598 under orders of Spain's King Philip II and runs south from the City Gate. During the First Spanish Period, the street was known as "The Street of the Governor." The British named it in 1763 in honor of King George III. There are over twenty-five restored or reconstructed buildings of architectural diversity. The scale of St. George Street has been thoughtfully preserved.

Genoply School House (right) *14 St. George Street:* Now known as the "Oldest School House," the Genoply House is the only surviving Second Spanish Period frame building in the old city. The house was built ca. 1788 by Juan Genoply, a Greek carpenter. The house remained in his family until 1904. It is believed that the building was used for educational purposes before the Civil War. In 1918, the Genoply House was the residence and shop of Thomas and Cora Kearns, the first to promote it as the Oldest Frame House in St. Augustine, and the first to call it the Oldest School House. In 1934, the house was sold to Walter B. Fraser, the city's mayor from 1934 to1942. A promoter of St. Augustine historical attractions including the Fountain of Youth (p. 90), he began marketing the house as the Oldest Wooden School House in the United States Museum. The back courtyard (bottom) provides an accurate sense of the scale of these early buildings.

Riberia House *22 St. George Street*: Riberia House is a reconstructed First Spanish Period home built on the foundation of Juan Riberia's original 1750s structure.

Gomez House *27 St. George Street*: Part of the Spanish Quarter Village, this reconstruction of a First Spanish Period, timber-framed house represents the home of Lorenzo Gomez, a Spanish foot soldier. The simple post-and-beam construction is made of native yellow pine with mortised and tenon joining.

Bernado Gonzales House *37 St. George Street*: Bernardo Gonzales was a Spanish cavalryman. This reconstruction of the original 1734 house is part of the Spanish Quarter Village.

Josef Salcedo House *42 St. George Street:* Josef Salcedo was a Spanish artillery captain. This reconstruction is built on the foundation of his original eighteenth-century house that stood on this location.

Avero House/Saint Photios Greek Orthodox Chapel *41 St. George Street:* This structure (above, right) is a reconstruction of a First Spanish Period Home (1735-43). It houses the Saint Photios Greek Orthodox National Shrine, a memorial to the first Greek settlers on the American continent, and interprets their contributions to the culture of the St. Augustine community. Saint Photios the Great was the Ecumenical Patriarch of Constantinople during the middle of the ninth century. The shrine was dedicated on February 10, 1985. Relics of three women saints were sealed within a cavity in the top of the altar table. The interior (below) features icons executed in the traditional Byzantine style. The paintings are frescoes, applied directly to the walls and dome of the shrine. The altar table is made of Italian Botticini marble with decorative mosaics.

de Mesa-Sanchez House *43 St. George Street* (1702-1763): The Colonial Spanish Quarter Village is a living history museum representing life in 1740s St. Augustine. The original house on this site was built by Antonio de Mesa prior to 1763. During the Second Spanish Period, Juan Sanchez enlarged the property to the rear (above, bottom) and added the second story.

Peso de Burgo-Pellicer Houses *57 St. George Street*: This reconstruction follows plans of a frame duplex originally built in the British Period ca. 1785 by Francisco Pellicer. Jose Peso de Burgo, a shopkeeper, lived in one side of the duplex. The houses in the complex such as the candle shop (above, bottom) were built on foundations of the original structures, and preserve their original scale.

Arivas House *46 St. George Street* (1710-1740): This restored Spanish colonial home features English, Spanish, and American architectural elements.

Rodriguez-Avero-Sanchez House *52 St. George Street* (1565-1764): Fernando Rodriguez, a sergeant in the Spanish army, built this house during the first Spanish occupation. Antonia Avero inherited it in 1762, but fled to Cuba before the British occupation. Twenty years later she couldn't reclaim the house. It was auctioned to Juan Sanchez in 1791.

Oliveros House 59 *St. George Street*: The original Oliveros house was built in 1798 and survived on this site until 1908. This reconstruction is now used as a cigar factory.

Benet Store 62 *St. George Street*: Pedro Benet, who lived across the street (p. 28), purchased the original building on this site in 1839. It was used as a store until the late 1800s. The building survived until 1903. This Second Spanish Period reconstruction is now a gift shop.

Villalonga House *72 St. George Street*: Reconstructed in 1976, this represents the home of Bartolmeo Villalonga (1789-1825), the son of Juan Villalonga, an early Minorcan land owner. The original house was built between 1815 and 1820.

Benet House *65 St. George Street*: The original late-Second Spanish Period residence was built ca. 1794 by Esteban Benet, a Minorcan émigré. His great-great grandsons Stephen Vincent Benet and William Rose Benet both won Pulitzer Prizes. The reconstruction is now an ice cream parlor.

Acosta House *74 St. George Street*: This historic reconstruction represents a house built between 1803 and 1812 by Jorge Acosta. Acosta, a Corsican, and his wife Margarita Villalonga, a Minorcan, were children of the New Smyrna Colony. The original coquina building was not demolished until ca. 1917. It was a private residence until the 1880s when it was used by the Women's Exchange in 1889. The reconstruction was dedicated in 1976.

Marin-Hassett House *97 St. George Street*: The Marin-Hassett House is a reconstruction of a First Spanish Period upper class home. Father Thomas Hassett, who arrived with the Minorcan colony at New Smyrna, owned the house in 1787.

Casa de Hidalgo *St. George and Hypolita Streets*: This reconstruction was built by the Spanish government in 1965 as a contribution to St. Augustine's four hundredth anniversary activities. It portrays a First Spanish Period gentleman's house in rural Spain. It was a cafe, but is now owned by the City of St. Augustine and will be incorporated into the heritage tourism experience as a reminder of the city's Spanish legacy and today's relationships with Spain.

Sanchez House *105 St. George Street:* The Sanchez House is a restoration of the structure built between 1807 and 1816 by Francisco Xavier Sanchez. One of the most successful planters in Florida, Sanchez derived his wealth from cattle and timber products. During the British Period (1763-1784), Sanchez served as a property agent for the Spanish monarchy during St. Augustine's transition to the British rule. During the Second Spanish Period (1784-1821) Sanchez helped reclaim property from the exiting British Government for the returning Spanish. The intermarriage of the Solana and Sanchez families with the Minorcan families began at this time and created the vast network of close family relations that exists in St. Augustine to this day.

The Pena-Peck House *143 St. George Street:* The Pena-Peck House was built in 1750 by order of the King of Spain to be the residence of his Royal Treasurer, Juan Esteban Pena. Built of native coquina stone, this house is the finest example of First Spanish Period homes in St. Augustine. During the British Period, it was leased to Dr. John Moultrie of Charleston, South Carolina. Moultrie became lieutenant governor of Florida. He added four fireplaces and the east wing.

Dr. Seth Peck and his family arrived from Connecticut in 1833. Dr. Peck purchased this house in 1837 and completely renovated it, adding a second story and demolishing the remains of the east wing. Dr. Peck's office was on the first floor (opposite, right). His family occupied the second floor, keeping their dining room on the first floor (opposite, left). The Peck family held title to the house for ninety-four years. Anna Burt, the last survivor of the family, willed the property to the city of St. Augustine in 1931. The Woman's Exchange, of which Anna Burt was a member, agreed to maintain the house and opened it to the public in 1932.

THE CITY CENTER AND PLAZA

Statue of Ponce de León (above): Ponce de León was the governor of the Spanish colony of Puerto Rico. In 1513, he began the voyage that would result in his discovery of Florida. Erected in 1923, this statue was a gift from Dr. Andrew Anderson. It is a copy of a statue in San Juan, Puerto Rico.

Government House (right, top): Buildings on this site have been used as the offices and residences of colonial governors for two hundred years. In 1690, the first wooden building was replaced by one of coquina, which burned in 1702. Remodeled in 1713, it was again used as the Governor's Palace. In 1935 it was further remodeled to resemble a structure in a 1734 British painting. Today, the Historic St. Augustine Preservation Board occupies the upper floors and the Museum of St. Augustine utilizes the first floor.

The Public Market (right, center): There have been public markets on this site since 1598. King Philip II of Spain decreed that all colonial towns should have a central plaza. On market day, the bell in the cupola announced to villagers that produce, meats, and fish were available for sale. The current open-air building was built in 1824.

Plaza de la Constitution (right, bottom): The plaza is named for the obelisk, seen in the distance, which commemorates the liberal Spanish constitution of 1812. To the right is the base of the Civil War Monument built in 1872.

King Street (above), seen here from the Bridge of Lions, is one of St. Augustine's main east-west thoroughfares. It forms the southern boundary of the city plaza. Many large buildings on King Street were converted into commercial buildings or boarding houses.

1 King Street: Built in 1888 and originally used as a dry goods store, this building has always been a retail center.

The Seth Wakeman House 9 *King Street*: A Territorial Era (1821-1845) building once stood on this site. The current structure is a reconstruction of a and Second Spanish Period colonial yle residence. It is now a retail center.

The Lyon Building 41 *King Street*: he Moorish Revival Lyon Building was uilt by contractor S. Bangs Manse in 886-7. The building has undergone ountless changes and has housed many usinesses such as the St. Augustine Gas nd Electric Company, the YMCA, a almist's studio, a pharmacy, and profes-onal offices.

First Union Bank Building: *24 Cathedral Street:* Built in 1926, the bank was designed by a local architect, Francis Hollingsworth, known for his Mediterranean Revival style.

The Basilica Cathedral: *38 Cathedral Place:* In 1788, Royal Engineer Mariano de la Rocque laid the groundwork for building a parish church adjacent to the Plaza. Begun in 1790, the neoclassical cathedral was completed and dedicated in 1797. A fire gutted the church in 1887. James Renwick, the architect for the reconstruction, added the bell tower. In the 1960s, the cathedral was stuccoed. The Basilica cathedral is one of the oldest Catholic religious buildings in the United States.

Cathedral Street looking west : On the left is the Old Market in the Plaza. In the middle of the photograph is the Basilica Cathedral. Rising above the cityscape is the First Union Bank Building.

Avenida Menéndez from the Bridge of Lions: Avenida Menéndez, once called Bay Street, is a major north-south artery that forms the eastern border of St. Augustine. This view shows the sea wall, Matanzas Bay, and the Castillo de San Marcos in the distance.

Espinoza-Sanchez House 44 *Avenida Menéndez/110 Charlotte*: Formerly known as the Pérez-Snow House, this late First Spanish Period house was built by Don Diego Espinoza, one of the city's prominent businessmen. The house was altered and restored numerous times, and survived two fires. The entrance on Charlotte Street (above, top) was added in the Second Spanish Period. The four arches are the only original First Spanish Period elements to survive. Mediterranean Revival details were added in 1963. The Exchange Bank purchased the property and sought to restore the building to its First Spanish Period style.

Carr House *46 Avenida Menéndez*: Juan Navarro built the original home on this site. It was rebuilt in 1850 by Burroughs E. Carr who gave it its Colonial Spanish architectural flavor. Destroyed by fire in 1887, it was rebuilt to its original appearance with concrete instead of coquina.

Casablanca Apartments *24 Avenida Menéndez*: In 1914, Gould T. Butler, a civil engineer and architect, designed this Mediterranean Revival building on the bay. Listed on the National Register of Historic Places, it is now a bed-and-breakfast.

Casa de la Paz *22 Avenida Menéndez*: Casa de la Paz was built during the Flagler Era in 1915 as a private residence for the Puller family. It has been a private home, a school, and a restaurant. It was converted to a bed-and-breakfast in 1986.

FLAGLER ERA ARCHITECTURE

The Hotel Ponce de León /Flagler College *King and Cordova Streets*:
Industrialist Henry Flagler built the extravagantly detailed Hotel
Ponce de León in 1888. Considered one of the finest examples of Spanish
Renaissance architecture in the United States, the design was a collabo-
ration between Bernard Maybeck and architects John M. Carrere and
Thomas Hastings. The interior was planned by Louis Tiffany. The hotel
was the first structure in the United States to use the poured concrete
technique developed by Franklin W. Smith. In 1967, it became the home
of Flagler College.

The entrance courtyard. Windows and doors feature elaborate terra-cotta and tile ornamentation.

A native of rural New York, Henry Morrison Flagler became one of the original partners in Standard Oil. When he arrived in St. Augustine in 1883, he was already a multi-millionaire. The statue of Henry Flagler at the entrance to Flagler College was built in 1915 and was moved to this site in the early 1970s.

The rotunda dome.

The main dining hall with architectural detailing designed by Louis Tiffany.

Alcazar Hotel/Lightner Museum *79 King Street*: The Spanish Renaissance Revival style Alcazar Hotel was Henry Flagler's second luxury hotel. The design by architects Carrere and Hastings was inspired by the royal palace in Seville, Spain. With its two large towers (opposite), ornate spires, and red tile roofs, the Alcazar reflects its Arabic name, Alkasr or "royal castle." The luxurious hotel featured spas, steam baths, a gymnasium, and the world's largest indoor swimming pool. The Great Depression brought an end to the hotel. In 1948, it was purchased by Otto Lightner, founder of *Hobbies* magazine. Lightner willed the building and his collection to the City of St. Augustine. The St. Augustine City Hall and the Lightner Museum now occupy the hotel.

The Casa Monica Hotel (The Cordova) 95 *Cordova*: This Moorish Revival hotel was built in 1887 by Boston architect Franklin W. Smith. After only three months as a hotelier, Smith sold the property to Henry Flagler who renamed it the Cordova. In 1902 the Cordova was connected to the Alcazar Hotel with a bridge. The facility was then known as the Alcazar Annex. The economic pressures of the Great Depression forced the closing of the hotel in 1932. In 1962, St. John's County acquired the Annex for use as its courthouse. In 1997, Richard C. Kessler purchased the building; two years later he reopened it as the luxurious Casa Monica Hotel.

Don Pedro Menéndez de Avilés: A bronze statue dedicated to St. Augustine's founding father, Don Pedro Menéndez de Avilés, is located in the front garden of the Lightner Museum courtyard, to the west of the Casa Monica. Erected in 1972, the statue was presented to the city by Mayor Fernando Juarez of Avilés, Spain, which is St. Augustine's sister city. In 1979, the garden was formally dedicated as the Parque de Menéndez.

Memorial Presbyterian Church *Valencia and Sevilla Streets:* Patterned after St. Mark's Cathedral in Venice, this splendid example of Venetian Renaissance architecture was built in 1889 and dedicated on March 16, 1890. Henry Flagler built the church as a memorial to his only daughter, Jenny Louise Benedict, who died at sea en route to St. Augustine. Both Flagler and his daughter are buried in the church.

The copper dome rises 150 feet overhead. The terra cotta frieze work was produced by Italian artisans.

The entrance arches are typical of the Venetian Renaissance style. The church is constructed of poured concrete walls and buttresses with no internal reinforcement. The gardens and grounds were donated in 1968 by Jean Flagler Mathews, Henry Flagler's granddaughter.

First Methodist Church *120 King Street*: The church was built in 1911 with a brick and stucco finish. Pointed arches, decorative brickwork, and pilasters mark its Gothic Revival style.

Grace United Methodist Church 8 *Carrere Street*: John M. Carrere and Thomas Hastings, while working on the Ponce de León Hotel, also produced this Spanish Renaissance church for Flagler. Built in 1887, it features salmon colored surfaces, cast terra-cotta decoration, with exposed concrete and shell aggregate. Flagler built this church for the Methodist community, who, in turn, ceded to him the land on which he would build the Alcazar Hotel.

Ancient City Baptist Church 27 *Sevilla Street*: This brown-brick Romanesque Revival style church was built in 1895. Henry Flagler offered the lot to the congregation. The design features a cone-shaped turret, a three-story tower, decorative brick ornamentation, and arched windows and entryway.

Casa Amarylla/Wiley Hall 6 *Valencia Street:* The two-and-a-half story, wood frame building was built in 1898. It is one of the best Colonial Revival style structures in the city. Its first resident was Dr. Fremont-Smith, a prominent physician from Maine who served as Flagler's hotel physician. In 1899 and 1900, Flagler sold the property to lumber magnate Albert Lewis, who lived there for over twenty years, calling it Casa Amarylla.

The house stood empty for most of the 1930s. In 1936, Louise Francis, Lewis's daughter-in-law, undertook a significant remodeling. Her plan was to use the house as a charitable preschool day care center. Architect Fred A. Hollingsworth oversaw the work. Mrs. Francis died before the project was completed. The nursery was not endowed in her will, and the building was sold.

Dr. Vernon A. Lockwood purchased the house and converted it into apartments. From 1940 to 1975, it was known as the Valencia Apartments.

The last private owner, Lawrence Lewis, Jr., Mrs. Francis's son, gave the property to Flagler College which now uses it as an administrative building.

Markland House *102 King Street*: Dr. Andrew Anderson began construction of this Colonial Revival structure in 1839. He did not live to see its completion in 1840. His son, Andrew, a friend of Flagler and also a physician, expanded and remodeled the house to its present form in 1901. Today, it houses offices and classrooms for Flagler Collage.

Schofield House *20 Valencia Avenue*: This masonry Victorian mansion was built between 1887 and 1891 for the first manager of the Ponce de León Hotel, Osborn Dunlap Seavey. The home was a typical winter residence for wealthy vacationers. The property was owned by Union Generals John McAllister Schofield (1899-1906) and Martin Hardin (1916-1923). In 1987, Flagler College completed a $500,000 restoration, salvaging as much original material as possible.

Ingraham House *32 Sevilla Street*: Flagler built this magnificent Colonial Revival mansion in 1894 for James Ingraham, one of his chief executives. Ingraham was vice president of the Florida East Coast Railway, president of the Model Land Company, and mayor of St. Augustine from 1915 to 1920. In 1924, after his death, Louise Wise Lewis, a Flagler heiress, became the owner. Mrs. Lewis later donated the home to the Memorial Presbyterian Church for use as their manse.

Villa Zorayda (Zorayda Castle) *83 King Street*: Franklin W. Smith, a hardware merchant and amateur architect, built the Villa Zorayda in 1851. Inspired by the Alhambra in Spain, and named for a princess in Washington Irving's *Tales of the Alhambra*, it was his first built project. His use of poured concrete inspired Flagler to use this new building technique for his hotels and churches. The keenly inventive Smith built the House of Pansa in Saratoga Springs, New York, a reproduction of one of Pompeii's lost buildings. The Moorish Revival Villa Zorayda features latticed windows, a variety of window shapes, Moorish arches decorated with Arabic relief and polychrome tiles, and recessed porches. In 1900, the villa was opened to the public as a tourist attraction. The villa was used as a restaurant, night club, a casino, and a hotel. Today, it is unoccupied.

ARCHITECTURE IN SOUTH ST. AUGUSTINE, INCLUDING THE "OLDEST HOUSE"

Paredas-Segui-McMillan House *224 St. George Street*: Built in 1764, the original coquina house had only one story. The wooden second story was added in 1823. The house received a major restoration in the 1960s.

Gingerbread House *232 St. George Street*: An example of Civil War-era Carpenter Gothic, the house was built ca. 1857. The J. Downing Stanbury family owned it from 1873 to 1923. The Gibson Family operated it as the Magnolia Inn until 1945. It is now a private residence.

Villa Flora *234 St. George Street*: n 1898, Rev. O. A. Weenolson built this Moorish-Romanesque Revival house as his winter residence. Made of coquina and yellow brick, it features extensive use of stained glass. It is now owned by the Sisters of St. Joseph.

St. Joseph Convent *243 St. George Street*: The Sisters of St. Joseph came to St. Augustine from Le Puy, France, in 1866. They built their convent in 1874-1876. The pointed window arches survive from the original structure which has been extensively remodeled through the years.

Murat House *250 St. George Street*: This Second Spanish Period house was built by Antonio Huertas in 1791. Emperor Napoleon's nephew, Prince Napoleon Achille Murat, built a plantation south of the city, and lived here in 1824. Ralph Waldo Emerson rented the house in the late 1820s. The Victorian balcony was added ca. 1880 by Amos Spear.

Bronson Cottage *252 St. George Street*: Bronson Cottage was designed in 1875 for Robert and Isabel Bronson by their friend, the eminent architect Andrew Jackson Davis. Favoring the Gothic Revival style, Davis was commissioned to design many state capitols. This is his only work in Florida. The house was sold in 1905 and used as a fine arts building by St. Joseph's Academy. It has recently been restored and is now a private residence.

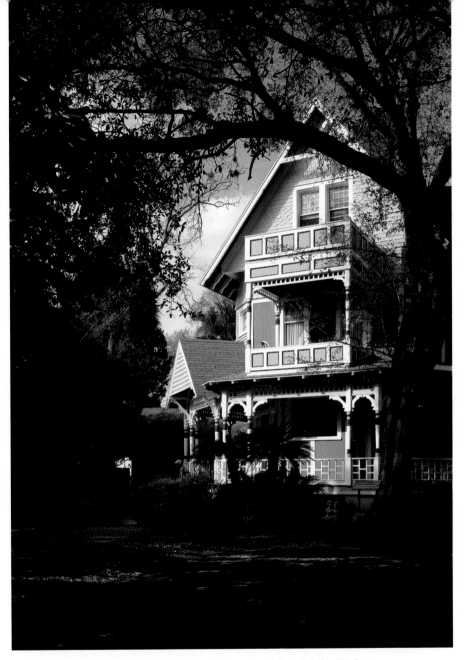

Upham Cottage *268 St. George Street*: Colonel John Upham, a career officer from Milwaukee, began construction on this Queen Anne residence in 1892. In spite of the mysterious drowning death of its contractor, the house was completed in 1894. It was the site of lavish St. Augustine society parties. Often used as an apartment house, it is once again a private home. The Queen Anne style features jigsawn rafters and brackets and lattice ornamentation on the roof gables. The present octagonal configuration is considerably different from the original design.

Segui-Kirby-Smith House *12 Avilés Street*: Bernardo Segui was an impoverished Minorcan survivor of the New Smyrna Colony; he ultimately became one of the wealthiest merchants in the city. Segui built this two-story house ca. 1800. In 1821, his widow, Aguada, leased it to Federal Judge Joseph Lee Smith, father of Edmund Kirby Smith, the last Confederate general to surrender. The building was the public library from 1896 to 1987. It is now the research library of the St. Augustine Historical Society.

Ximenez-Fatio House *20 Avilés Street*: Andreas Ximenez, a merchant, built this coquina stone house in 1798. It underwent renovations in 1830 when Margaret Cook purchased it and ran it as a boarding house, one of the few socially acceptable business ventures for a nineteenth-century woman. In 1855, it was purchased by Louisa Fatio who ran it as an inn and tourist destination. In 1939, the house was acquired by The National Society of The Colonial Dames of America in The State of Florida and opened to the public as an historic museum house. The house was placed on the National Register of Historic Places in 1973 and is one of the best restored of St. Augustine's colonial-era buildings.

Owner's Parlor (above): Hotel guests visited this elegant room by invitation only. The astral lamp cast a circle of light and permitted events to go on after dark. The painted canvas rug protected the floor from wear. The rug was coated with twenty-five to thirty layers of shellac, which gave it a texture and durability similar to linoleum.

Kitchen (opposite, above): The house kitchen is the oldest existing kitchen in St. Augustine. Much of the work of the house, including cooking, washing, and laundry, took place in this detached building. The kitchen fireplace had to be large enough to accommodate roasts and other preparations for twenty to thirty guests. The smaller domed opening to the right was used for baking bread.

Dining Room (opposite, below): A widely acclaimed dining room was essential to establishing the reputation of a hotel. This one served three meals a day to thirty guests, and was celebrated for its cuisine. The availability of fresh seafood, fruits, and vegetables impressed guests, especially those on holiday from the north.

Solana House *21 Avilés Street*: Don Manuel Solana, a Minorcan merchant, built this house around 1800. The architecture is a blend of English and Spanish elements. It is now operated as a bed and breakfast.

O'Reilly House *32 Avilés Street*: Built before 1763, the house became the property of Don Miguel (Michael) O'Reilly in 1783. He later willed the house to the Catholic Church. The Sisters of St. Joseph lived and taught in the house starting in 1866, and restored it in the 1940s. It is now open to the public.

Gaspar Papi/Don Toledo House *36 Avilés Street*: This coquina stone house was built in the early 1800s by Minorcan Gaspar Papi, a survivor of the New Smyrna colony. Later it was referred to as the Don Toledo House and "Whitney's Oldest House." It is now owned by the Sisters of St. Joseph.

Fontane House (above) *33 Avilés Street*:

It is believed that this two-story, post and beam wooden building was built around 1835, possibly earlier. This makes it one of the earliest Territorial Period residences in the city. Typical of the period, the house was built on the street line. "It was called the Ben Bow Tavern in the 1920s and the Fireside Artcrafters, as well as the Blue Gate Gift Shop, in the 1930s. It was converted from a store to efficiency apartments in the mid-1950s. It has since been purchased for use as a residence and restoration project. The modern modifications have been removed.

Kenwood Inn (opposite, above) *38 Marine Street*: Built between 1865 and 1885, the Kenwood Inn was first advertised as a boarding house in 1866 and has welcomed visitors ever since. It is now a bed and breakfast.

Marin House (opposite, center) *47 Marine Street*: Located behind the Hopkins-Belknap Cottage on Avenida Menéndez, the Colonial Era Marin House was built around 1791. Francisco Marin, one of the members of the Minorcan colony, acquired the house and lot in the 1780s. Captain Henry Belknap bought the Victorian cottage that stood at 142 Avenida Menéndez and began to make wooden additions to it.

Puello House (opposite, below) *53 Marine Street*: The Puello House was built between 1812 and 1821. The Mediterranean Revival house has been completely restored and is now a private residence.

Gonzales-Jones House *56 Marine Street*: This First Spanish Period house was built around 1702. It has been restored and is a private residence.

St. Francis Barracks *82 Marine Street:* Missionaries constructed a wooden convent on this site between 1724 and 1737. The site contained only log and palm thatch buildings which ultimately rotted or burned. The convent was abandoned when Florida came under British rule in 1763. The British converted it into military barracks, and it functioned as such through the Second Spanish Period. In 1821, the U.S. Army took over the complex. During the Civil War it housed first Confederate, and later, Union troops, and finally, men of the regular army artillery. It was abandoned as a military post by the national government in 1900. The complex was leased to the Florida National Guard in 1907 and formally given to them in 1921 by an act of Congress.

King's Bakery *97 Marine Street*: This is the only remaining structure from the British period. It was built near the barracks to provide fresh bread for the troops. It now serves as offices and garages for the military personnel of the barracks.

Barracks Houses *90, 92, 96 Marine Street*: The one and one-half story Frame Vernacular housing complex was built between 1865 and 1885. They are among the oldest buildings in the area. Architectural details typical of the style are the chamfered posts on the two-story porch and the jig sawn railing. The houses were built for the officers of the military compound.

"The Oldest House"

Gonzales-Alvarez House/"The Oldest House" *14 St. Francis Street*:
Archaeologists can show continuous occupancy of this house from the early 1600s. The first palm thatch and log structure built on this site was probably burned in 1702. A two-room, one-story coquina stone structure was built in the early 1700s. The Tomas Gonzales family lived here for forty years until Florida was ceded to England in 1763 and the town's three thousand Spanish residents had to leave. British Major Joseph Peavett purchased the house and began the series of alterations and additions that have brought the once small structure to its present form. In 1790, the house was auctioned off to Spaniard Geronimo Alvarez. He and his descendants lived here for nearly one hundred years. Over the next forty years, it was home to various occupants, including those who first opened it to the public as "The Oldest House in the United States." The Saint Augustine Historical Society acquired the house in 1918. It was designated a National Historic Landmark in 1970.

The second story is typical of British-era additions to First Spanish Period houses. The gardens contain plants similar to those grown by Spanish, British, and American occupants.

"Maria's Room": The British-era dining room/bedroom suite is furnished much as it was when Maria Peavett used it.

The kitchen outbuilding, is a twentieth-century reproduction; but it is a reminder that in many early American houses the kitchen was often placed in a separate building, to reduce the risk of fire and, in the South, to keep the main house cooler.

The Tavern: This recreation of a British-era tavern features an indoor fireplace, a typical British addition in the 1700s.

Tovar House *22 St. Francis Street*: Built around 1791, it was originally a one-story masonry building. The second story was added during the British Period. It is now owned and operated by the St. Augustine Historical Society.

Fernandez-Llambias House *31 St. Francis Street*: Pedro Fernandez built a one-story, two room house on this site in 1763. The loggia was added during the British Period, and the second floor and balcony during the Second Spanish Period. The Llambias family purchased the house in 1854 and occupied it until 1919. The house was restored in 1954 by architect Stuart Barnette.

The St. Francis Inn *279 St. George Street*: Built in 1791, this Second Spanish Colonial Period house was first owned by Gaspar Garcia, a sergeant in the Third Battalion of the Infantry Regiment of Cuba. In 1802, it was purchased by sea captain Juan Ruggiers. In 1838, Col. Thomas Henry Dummett of Barbados bought the house. Upon his death in 1845, his daughter Anna converted the house into a lodge. Philanthropist John L. Wilson purchased the inn in 1888 and made extensive renovations including a third floor and the mansard roof. The inn's visitors included many literary figures such as publisher Aaron Jones; authors Dr. William Hayne Simmons, Verle Pope, and Gladys Hasty Carroll; and the Pulitzer Prize winning historian Van Wycks Brooks. Through the years the inn was known as the Teahan House, the Hudson House, the Valencia Annex, the Amity Apartments, the Salt Air Apartments, the Palms, and the Graham House. It was christened the St. Francis Inn in 1948.

First Baptist Parsonage *89 St. Francis Street:* In 1872, a group of African Americans in St. Augustine established their congregation. In 1893, they built their church on this site. A fire destroyed the church in 1915, but the congregation rebuilt it in 1916. The First Baptist Church hosted rallies with Dr. Martin Luther King, Jr. in 1963 and 1964.

St. Benedict the Moor *Martin Luther King and St. Francis Streets:* Before the establishment of this church in 1898, African American Catholics in St. Augustine received ministration from the cathedral clergy and the Sisters of St. Joseph. Many of the early parishioners were servants of Spanish settlers whose faith they adopted. Today, St. Benedict the Moor has a multi-racial congregation of about four hundred people.

Sons of Israel Synagogue *161 Cordova Street*: Jews were participants in the earliest settlements in Florida and St. Augustine. Converted Jews may have come with Ponce de León when he landed in Florida in 1513. One of his leaders, Pedro Menéndez Marques, was a Marrano. Moses Levy purchased part of the Arrendondo grant in the early 1800s. This became the site of Fort Mose, the first free black community in the United States. His son David Yulee (nee Levy) was the first Jew elected to the U.S. Senate. The Congregation Sons of Israel was organized in the nineteenth century under the leadership of Jacob Tarlinsky. Until 1923, when this synagogue was built, services were conducted in a private home on Bridge Street. Most members were Russian and Eastern European Jews seeking freedom from religious and social persecution. In 1925, the first rabbi was hired and formal classes in Hebrew were given.

Star General Store *Cordova and Bridge Streets*: Built ca.1899-1904, this original residence housed a kindergarten, a doll and toy store, and a millinery shop before undergoing conversion into two apartments for women of the de Medicis family in 1921. It is part of the Old St. Augustine Village complex.

Bayfront Westcott House *146 Avenida Menéndez*: This Victorian mansion was built in the Flagler era for Dr. John Westcott in the late 1880s. Dr. Westcott, after moving to St. Augustine in 1858, became a prominent citizen with interests in transportation and politics. The St. Johns Railroad, whose tracks spread from the San Sebastian River to Tocoi, was one of his first accomplishments. Dr. Westcott is also known for his involvement in the development of the Intercoastal Waterway linking the St. Johns River to Miami.

Brooks Villa *174 Avenida Menéndez*: This example of the late Moorish Revival style was built in 1891 for Charles S. and Tracy Brooks. It lacks a Moorish ornamental parapet, but has the horseshoe arches and ornamental tile work typical of the style. The columns under the arches are similar to those of the Alcazar Hotel. It was owned by author/lecturer Dr. Maurice Leahy in the 1960s.

CEMETERIES

Huguenot Cemetery *Orange Street*: St. Augustine's Protestants were buried on Anastasia Island during the late Spanish period. When Florida became a U.S. possession, there developed a need for a Protestant cemetery. The city gained access to a half-acre plot to serve as a resting place for non-Catholics. In 1832, the land was transferred to the trustees of the Presbyterian Church. The cemetery was often called the Public Burial Grounds to avoid the mistaken belief that Huguenots massacred in 1565 were buried there.

Tolomato Cemetery *Cordova and Orange Streets*: This cemetery, where Christian Indians were buried, is named for the church and village of Tolomato, an Indian village noted on a map from 1737. Unused by the British, it was again in use when the Spanish returned. The cemetery was closed in 1884. Those interred here include the Most Reverend Jean Pierre Augustin Marcellin Verot, the first bishop of St. Augustine, and Father Feliz Verela, a vicar-general of New York.

ARCHITECTURE IN NORTH ST. AUGUSTINE, INCLUDING THE FOUNTAIN OF YOUTH

Dismukes House *80 Water Street:* This splendid Queen Anne residence is one of the oldest brick homes in St. Augustine. It was built in 1890 for banker John T. Dismukes; it remained in his family for thirty years. Dismukes established the First National Bank of St. Augustine, and was the president of the Peoples Bank for Savings. The house is located just north of the historic district off San Marco Avenue.

Castle Warden (now Ripley's Believe It or Not! Museum) *19 San Marco Avenue:* This Moorish Revival castle, the largest poured concrete residence in the city, was built in 1887 by the St. Augustine Improvement Company. It was the winter residence of William G. Warden, a partner in Standard Oil. In 1941, it was purchased by Norton Baskin who remodeled it as the Castle Warden Hotel. Mr. Baskin's wife was the Pulitzer Prize-winning novelist Marjorie Kinnan Rawlings. Baskin sold the hotel in 1946. It remained a hotel until 1950 when it became the now famous Ripley's Believe It or Not! Museum.

Mission of Nombre de Dio *30 Ocean Avenue*: On September 8, 1565, Pedro Menéndez de Avilés proclaimed this site for Spain and the Church. Menéndez knelt here to kiss a wooden cross presented to him by Father Francisco Lopez de Mendoza Grajales, the chaplain of his expedition. On these grounds, Father Lopez celebrated the first parish Mass, and Spanish settlers began their devotion to Our Lady of la Leche. It has been called "America's Most Sacred Acre." The Mission is located north of the historic district off San Marco Avenue.

The lagoon is named for Father Lopez. The two hundred foot high Great Cross, seen in the background, was erected as a memorial of the Four Hundredth Anniversary of the Mission.

The Spanish title for the statue of Mary nursing the infant Jesus was *Nuestra Senora del la Leche y buen parto* (Our Lady of the Milk and Happy Delivery). A shrine to Our Lady of la Leche was first built in 1616. The present building, the fourth on this site, was erected in 1914. It is a replica of the earlier coquina chapels. It houses a replica of the statue of Our Lady of la Leche.

The Fountain of Youth National Archaeological Park

This unique park is located where Spanish conquistadors first came ashore in what is now the continental United States. When they landed, the priest who had accompanied the soldiers said a Mass of thanksgiving as the native Timucua Indians looked on. Ponce de León took possession of the continent for Spain, naming it "La Florida" to commemorate the Easter season and the blossom-filled coastline he encountered. With the landing of Ponce de León, Spanish claim to Florida was established. Ponce de León's claim, in effect, covered all of America from Florida to Labrador, from coast to coast.

Important archaeological discoveries at the park include Ponce de León's recording landmark and accompanying artifacts; the first Christian Indian burials in North America with Mission Period interments; Timucua Indian hut foundations and relics; artifacts indicating Timucua habitation for more than one thousand years prior to Ponce de León's arrival; and evidence that Pedro Menéndez's colony occupied the site during the sixteenth century. Current archaeological excavations, directed by Dr. Kathleen Deagan, search for the foundation of the first wooden fort built by the Spanish and the first Catholic mission constructed on the site. The entrance to the park is located on Myrtle Street off San Marco Avenue north of the historic district.

The anchor and cannon (left) were salvaged off the coast of Cape Canaveral and are believed to have been from Jean Ribault's ill-fated French fleet which went down in a hurricane in 1565. The large clay jars are early Spanish water urns called tinajones. They were placed under the eaves of houses to catch rain water. They weigh over eight hundred pounds and are over three hundred years old.

Ponce de León (p. 93) found a prehistoric Indian spring (following page) he hoped would be the Fountain of Youth. The spring still flows and visitors are invited to sample the waters.

He marked the spot by leaving a stone cross in the ground (below). The cross consists of twenty-seven stone slabs—fifteen in the staff and thirteen in the beam—to indicate the year of his visit, 1513. The cross remains in its original place.

THE LIGHTHOUSE

Lighthouse Keeper's House 81 *Lighthouse Avenue*: The two-story brick building was home to lighthouse keepers and their families from its construction in 1876 until 1955 when the lighthouse was automated. The house was built as a duplex. The head keeper and his family lived on the north side; the assistant on the south side. Unlike most Florida buildings, the house had a basement with two cisterns which held drinking water collected from rainwater off the roof. In the 1960s, the Light Station was vacated and the house fell victim to neglect and vandalism. In 1980, The Junior Service League of St. Augustine began a massive restoration to save the station. The house was restored to its original Victorian elegance.

The Lighthouse (p. 96):

The Spanish built a watchtower on this site at the end of the sixteenth century. In 1824, a tower and beacon became Florida's first official lighthouse. Coastal erosion threatened this tower, which eventually fell into the sea during a storm in 1880. Work on the current tower began in 1871. It is constructed of Alabama brick, Philadelphia iron, and Georgia granite. Rising 165 feet above sea level, it is St. Augustine's oldest surviving brick structure. Originally, the light was powered by lard oil stored in the fuel storage house attached to the base of the tower. Kerosene later replaced the lard. The lighthouse was finally powered by electricity in 1936. Today it is powered by a one thousand-watt light bulb that can be seen for 19 to 25 nautical miles. The original 1874 Fresnel lens with 370 hand-cut prisms is still in the tower. The lighthouse is located on Anastasia Island off Anastasia Boulevard at the end of Old Beach Road.